Stepping into Freedom
A Christ-Centered Twelve-Step Program

Workbook

By Jimmy Ray Lee, D.Min.

Communications should be addressed to:
Living Free Ministries, Inc.
P. O. Box 22127
Chattanooga, TN 37422-2127

Scripture taken from the *Holy Bible, New International Version.*® Copyright ©1972, 1978, 1984 by International Bible Society. Used by permission of Zondervan Publishing House.

©Living Free, 1993, 1999. All rights reserved.

All rights are reserved. No part of the material protected by this copyright notice may be reproduced or utilized in any form or by any means, electronic or mechanical, including photocopying, recording, or any information storage and retrieval system, without written permission from the Living Free Ministries.

10 ISBN: 1-58119-040-9
13 ISBN: 978-1-58119-040-3

The Road to **Hope**, **Faith**, and **Freedom**

Cover Design: Graphic Advertising
Layout: Louise Lee

About the Author

Dr. Jimmy Ray Lee is the founder and president emeritus of Living Free Ministries, Inc. He is the author of *Understanding the Times* and several small group studies published by Living Free Ministries. Under the direction and guidance of Dr. Lee, Living Free Ministries produced Living Free—a high impact, video-based training. This training helps churches develop Christ-centered small groups that deal with the contemporary problems that people face today.

Dr. Lee is the founder and honorary chairman of Project 714 (now known as National Center for Youth Issues), a chemical prevention/intervention program for schools. He also founded an inner-city ministry called Ark Ministries that reached 600 to 700 young people weekly. He started the Chattanooga Teen Challenge and served as its president for three years. Jimmy served as Nashville Teen Challenge executive director during its formative years.

In 1983 he was awarded the "Service to Mankind Award" presented by the Highland Sertoma Club in Hixson, Tennessee.

Twelve Steps of Alcoholics Anonymous

1. Admitted we were powerless over alcohol—that our lives had become unmanageable.

2. Came to believe that a Power greater than ourselves could restore us to sanity.

3. Made a decision to turn our will and our lives over to the care of God *as we understood Him.*

4. Made a searching and fearless moral inventory of ourselves.

5. Admitted to God, to ourselves and to another human being the exact nature of our wrongs.

6. Were entirely ready to have God remove all these defects of character.

7. Humbly asked Him to remove our shortcomings.

8. Made a list of all persons we had harmed and became willing to make amends to them all.

9. Made direct amends to such people wherever possible, except when to do so would injure them or others.

10. Continued to take personal inventory and when we were wrong, promptly admitted it.

11. Sought through prayer and meditation to improve our conscious contact with God as *we understood Him,* praying only for knowledge of His will for us and the power to carry that out.

12. Having had a spiritual awakening as the result of these steps, tried to carry this message to alcoholics and to practice these principles in all our affairs.

The Twelve Steps are reprinted and adapted with permission of Alcoholics Anonymous World Services, Inc. Permission to reprint and adapt the Twelve Steps does not mean that AA has reviewed or approved the content of this publication nor that AA agrees with the views expressed herein. AA is a program of recovery from alcoholism. Use of the Twelve Steps in connection with programs and activities which are patterned after AA but which addresses other problems does not imply otherwise.

Stepping into Freedom
A Christ-Centered Twelve-Step Program

Contents

	Page
Introduction	2
The Twelve Steps of Wholeness	4
Orientation	6
Session 1 — Admitting My Powerlessness	12
Session 2 — Acknowledging My Belief in Jesus Christ	17
Session 3 — Affirming My Need for the Care of God	24
Session 4 — Auditing My Life	30
Session 5 — Accounting for My Actions	36
Session 6 — Agreeing with God	43
Session 7 — Abandoning My Sins	49
Session 8 — Amending My Ways	55
Session 9 — Acting on My Amends	62
Session 10 — Analyzing My Walk with Christ	68
Session 11 — Anchoring My Walk with Christ	73
Session 12 — Advancing My Faith in Christ	79
References	87

Workbook: *Stepping Into Freedom*, Living Free, P. O. Box 22127, Chattanooga, TN 37422-2127

Introduction

Welcome to *Stepping into Freedom*. This is a twelve-step approach to becoming free in Christ. The twelve steps used in *Stepping into Freedom* are taken from "The Twelve Steps of Wholeness" by Dr. Gary R. Sweeten.

He explains:

> Following a tradition of the early church and the Wesley revival, the Oxford Group systematized a series of "steps" as a process of cleansing one's inner life. These "steps" were later adapted by Alcoholics Anonymous with much of the Christian basis ignored. They are here re-adapted emphasizing this great Christian base so integral to the wholeness sought. Here the center of wholeness is recognized as the Lord Jesus Christ. The "steps" have also been changed to conform to other principles of discipleship and Christian growth.

The purpose of *Stepping into Freedom* is to help you develop roots and steadfastness in Christ so you can confidently master the problems you encounter. *Stepping into Freedom* will benefit anyone who wants to "grow in the grace and knowledge of our Lord and Savior Jesus Christ" (2 Peter 3:18).

Stepping into Freedom is not a substitute for medical or psychological care. We never advise anyone to stop taking medication or cancel a physician's care.

Stepping into Freedom can be used as a bible study for any life-controlling problem—anything that masters a person's life (substance, behavior or relationship). Just fill in the blank—drugs, alcohol, sex, gambling, co-dependency, etc. Actually, *Stepping into Freedom* will benefit anyone who wants to mature in Christ.

Please be faithful in your attendance at each group meeting and do the assignments in your workbook before each group session. There is a Step-by-Step Diary page for you to record your thoughts after each session.

May the Lord bless you and keep His hand on you.

Stepping into Freedom can be used as a bible study for any life-controlling problem—anything that masters a person's life . . . . Just fill in the blank.

Workbook: *Stepping Into Freedom*, Living Free, P. O. Box 22127, Chattanooga, TN 37422-2127

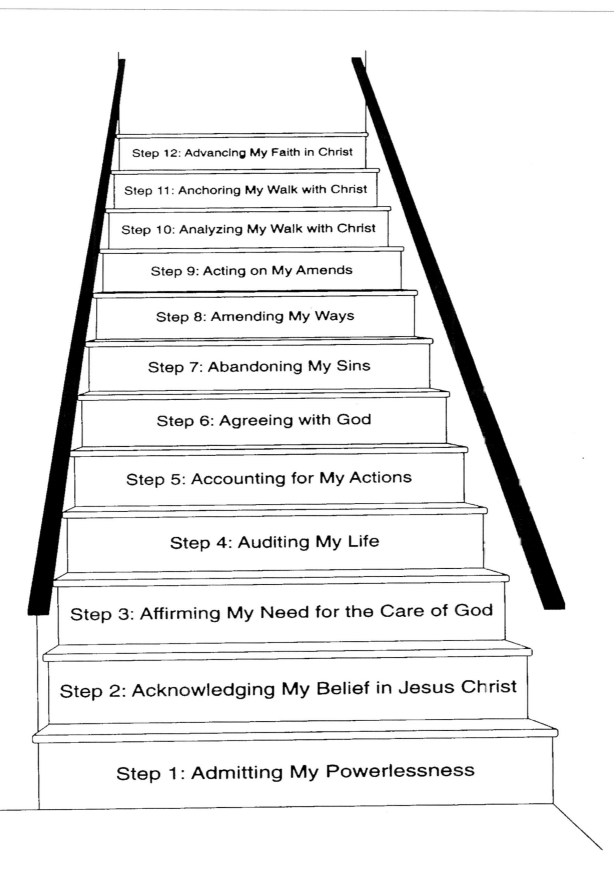

Workbook: *Stepping Into Freedom*, Living Free, P. O. Box 22127, Chattanooga, TN 37422-2127

The Twelve Steps of Wholeness

If a Christian will vigorously apply these principles and make these decisions, that person will move toward *Teleios*—wholeness in Christ.

1. I now see that I, of myself, am powerless—unable to control (manage) my life by myself.
Romans 7 and 8 Romans 7:18-19 Psalm 32:3-7
Romans 3:9-10, 23

2. I now realize that my Creator, God the Father, Son, and Holy Spirit, can restore me to wholeness in Christ.
Psalm 27:4-5 Mark 10:26-27 Philippians 2:13
Romans 8:9 Ezekiel 36:27

3. I now make a conscious decision to turn my entire will and life over to the care and direction of Jesus Christ as Teacher, Healer, Savior, and Lord.
Joshua 1:8-9 Jeremiah 29:11-14 Jeremiah 32:27
John 14:6 John 10:30 Mark 10:27
Matthew 28:18, 20b

4. Having made this decision, I now obey God's call in Scripture to make a fearless, ethical, moral, and scriptural inventory of my entire life in order to uncover all sins, mistakes, and character defects and to make a written list of every item uncovered.
Psalm 139:23-24 Lamentations 3:40 Jeremiah 23:24
Romans 8:26-27

5. After completing this inventory, I now will to "walk in the light, as he is in the light" (1 John 1:7) by admitting to myself, to God, and to at least one other person in Christ the exact nature of these wrongs.
Psalm 119:9-11 Acts 13:38-39 1 Timothy 1:15
James 5:13-16 Ephesians 5:13-14 Hebrews 9:14
1 John 1:7 Acts 2:37-38

6. Having agreed with God about my sinful behavior, I now ask for His forgiveness through Christ and openly acknowledge that I am forgiven according to Scripture.
James 4:10 1 John 1:8-9 1 John 2:1-2
Psalm 27:13-14 Psalm 118:18, then 17

7. I now repent (turn away) from all these behaviors in thought, word, and deed and ask God to remove each besetting sin through Jesus Christ.
John 5:14 John 8:10-11 Job 11:13-19
Ezekiel 18:30-32 Romans 5 and 6 Romans 12:1-2
1 John 2:3-6 2 Corinthians 10:5 Colossians 3:17

8. I now make a list of all persons I have harmed in thought, word, and deed and a list of all persons I believe have harmed me, and I will to make amends to all of them.
Ephesians 4:29-32 Hosea 11:1-4 Ephesians 5:1-2
Luke 6:31 Matthew 5:43-44 Matthew 18:15
Leviticus 19:17-18 Mark 12:31 Matthew 5:9

Workbook: *Stepping Into Freedom*, Living Free, P. O. Box 22127, Chattanooga, TN 37422-2127

9. I now go directly to these persons to forgive and to seek forgiveness, reconciliation, restitution, or release whenever and with whomever possible, unless to do so would cause further harm.
Matthew 5:23-24   Isaiah 1:18-20

10. I now consciously and prayerfully continue to "walk in the light" by unceasingly taking personal inventory of all my temptations and sins and, by keeping a constantly open relationship with God, myself, and other persons.
Matthew 26:41   James 1:13-15   Matthew 6:11-13
Proverbs 30:8-9   Ephesians 5:15-18   Ephesians 4:22-28
Psalm 4:3-5   Psalm 55:22   1 Peter 5 6-7
Colossians 3:13

11. I now continue in regular Scripture study, prayer, worship, and fellowship to increase God's will in my life.
Acts 2:42   Mark 12:28-33   Matthew 6:33
Psalm 89:15   Joshua 1:8   1 Kings 8 56-61
Colossians 3:12-17

12. Recognizing the impact of God in my life, I now intentionally share these principles and their effect with others as God's Spirit leads, and will to practice these principles in all areas of my life.
Micah 6:8   Ephesians 5:8   Psalm 40:8-10
Galatians 5:1   Revelation 12:11   2 Corinthians 3:17
Ephesians 6:10-18

The author is grateful to Dr. Gary R. Sweeten for the use of "The Twelve Steps of Wholeness." The material is published by permission of:

Dr. Gary R. Sweeten
Lifeway Centers
4015 Executive Park Drive
Suite 305
Cincinnati, Ohio 45241
513-769-4600

Workbook: *Stepping Into Freedom*, Living Free, P. O. Box 22127, Chattanooga, TN 37422-2127

Orientation

Personal Preparation: Getting Ready for Orientation

Welcome

Personal Notes

Welcome to *Stepping into Freedom*. You have taken a positive step. We thank God for you.

During this course, there will be suggested time alone with God in meditation, prayer, and scripture reading. This time with God is vital to being free in Jesus Christ. We encourage you to be faithful in your devotion time with the Lord.

Self-Awareness

A *Stepping into Freedom* group is a small group (usually fewer than 12 people) who want to better understand how they can maintain a life free from mastering problems by developing steadfastness in Christ.

It is our goal to begin a process of *building strength* into our lives. The problems are not going to disappear magically, but we will develop the strength to deal with them. Christ will help us overcome the obstacles we face. Our goal over the next few weeks will not be problem maintenance, but transformation through Christ.

The elements of a typical meeting are next.

Workbook: *Stepping Into Freedom*, Living Free, P. O. Box 22127, Chattanooga, TN 37422-2127

Meeting Format

Introduction: First we will pray together. Prayer is always appropriate during our meetings, especially as we begin our time together. After we begin with prayer, we will then spend a few minutes talking together and getting to know each other better. We hope this will grow to be a group of caring and supportive friends, but in any of our conversations here, you should never feel pressured to talk. We only want you to speak when you feel comfortable speaking.

Self-Awareness: Next in our meeting comes something we call our "Self-Awareness" time. This part of our meeting is designed to help us take a look at our life and better understand the pitfalls and delusion that accompanies life controlling problems. During Self-Awareness (about 20 minutes), we will discuss some of the practical issues involved in understanding and dealing with those troubled relationships.

Spiritual-Awareness: After our Self-Awareness time, we are going to open our Bibles and dig deep into the promises of God's Word. We are going to study about how God wants to work in our lives and in the lives of those we care about.

Application: After our bible study, we will take some time to work on applying what we have learned. God's Word has a lot to say to us where we are right now, and we are going to learn how to apply that truth to the decisions and actions of our daily lives.

During all of these parts of our meeting, we will have opportunities to minister to each other. God has given each of us the resource of other caring Christians. All through His Word, He reminds us of the valuable ministry we can have to one another, and we are going to see that kind of ministry to each other begin to happen through this group.

Workbook: *Stepping Into Freedom*, Living Free, P. O. Box 22127, Chattanooga, TN 37422-2127

Ground Rules

1. **We want you to be here.** Make every effort to attend each meeting. Make these 13 sessions a top priority in your life. Each session is important to you, and you are important to this group. In addition to what God wants to do in your life, you have a great deal to contribute to the lives of others in this group. If you must miss a meeting for some reason, please give us a call to let us know.

2. **You should speak within your own comfort level.** This has already been mentioned, but it is important that you consider the group meeting a nonthreatening place. Think about the questions that are asked. Some of you will be ready answer right away, but others it may take a while before you are comfortable. Do not feel pressured.

3. **There is to be confidentiality concerning anything that is shared within the group.** We must be able to trust each other to maintain confidentiality. It is never appropriate to gossip. (The only exception to maintaining confidentiality should be when a person is a danger to themselves or to others.)

4. **Make a commitment to prepare for each session.** Your group member workbook contains some written questions and Bible reading assignments that will get you ready for what we will be doing during our sessions here. Your workbook is a private place—just between you and God. No one else ever needs to read what you have written there. Do take time to let God work in your life during the week as you prepare for our time together.

5. **Spend time alone with God every day.** Included in each introduction section are some suggestions for how you might spend approximately 30 minutes a day in Bible reading, meditating on God's Word, and prayer. That time alone with God could be the most significant element of the healing and building God wants to do in your life.

6. **Keep in mind that this group is not a substitute for medical or psychological care.** We never advise anyone to stop taking prescribed medications or cancel their doctor's care.

Orientation

Workbook: *Stepping Into Freedom*, Living Free, P. O. Box 22127, Chattanooga, TN 37422-2127

In each session our spiritual awareness will be based on biblical principles which emphasize spiritual growth in Christ as the means to ongoing freedom from life-controlling problems. Colossians 2:6-8 serves as the launching pad for the 12 sessions that follow. Let's read the text together.

> So then, just as you received Christ Jesus as Lord, continue to live in him, rooted and built up in him, strengthened in the faith as you were taught, and overflowing with thankfulness.
>
> See to it that no one takes you captive through hollow and deceptive philosophy, which depends on human tradition and the basic principles of this world rather than on Christ.

What does this say to you about being spiritually aware?

Spiritual-Awareness

We will use the Apostle Paul's instructions in Colossians 2:6-8 as the launching pad for the *Stepping into Freedom* group.

Colossians 2:6
Paul emphasizes the need for continuity in Christ.

How does a person receive Christ? (See Ephesians 2:8-9.)

Why is God's grace and faith in Christ important in your desire to be mature in Christ?

Colossians 2:7
Paul encourages us to be "rooted and built up in him, strengthened in the faith . . . and overflowing with thankfulness."

Describe in your own words the four-phase process listed by Paul:

1. **Rooted.**
2. **Built up in Him.**
3. **Strengthened in the faith.**
4. **Overflowing with thankfulness.**

Colossians 2:8
Paul warns against deceptive philosophy.

In view of this verse, why is it important to guard against vain intellectualism and human philosophy as the means to your wholeness instead of Christ?

God's grace and faith in Christ are the foundation for the 12 sessions that will follow. Our goal is to begin in Christ (salvation) and continue (mature) in Christ.

Orientation   Workbook: *Stepping Into Freedom*, Living Free, P. O. Box 22127, Chattanooga, TN 37422-2127

Application

In John 8:31-32 Jesus told the believing Jews, "If you hold to my teaching, you are really my disciples. Then you will know the truth, and the truth will set you free."

In view of these verses, how can you maintain a life of living free in Christ?

Dr. Mike Chapman describes three principles of faith for living daily in Christ:

1. Faith is an *affirmation*. It is our AMEN that God's Word is 100 percent truth.

2. Faith is an *action*. Our convictions must lead to actions. We all live what we believe, not what we say we believe. "Faith without deeds is dead" (James 2:26).

3. Faith is an *attitude*. It is a calmness of spirit that comes from knowing that God is actively involved in our everyday lives. Faith is an attitude of peace in the midst of the storm. It is not a Hollywood or psychological fad or something you work up but God's goodness, wisdom, and power working in our lives (Lee, *Godly Heroes*, p. 78).

"And without faith it is impossible to please God, because anyone who comes to him must believe that he exists and that he rewards those who earnestly seek him" (Hebrews 11:6).

Session 1: Admitting My Powerlessness

Personal Preparation: Getting Ready for Session One

Step 1 I now see [admit] that I, of myself, am powerless, unable to control [manage] my life by myself.

Welcome

Personal Notes

Take 30 minutes each day to be alone with God in meditation and prayer. Read Romans 7 and 8.

Self-Awareness

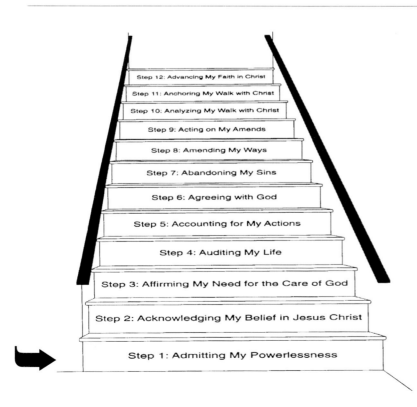

Session 1 — Workbook: *Stepping Into Freedom*, Living Free, P. O. Box 22127, Chattanooga, TN 37422-2127

In this session our goal is to help each other admit our powerlessness over a life-controlling problem. (A life-controlling problem is anything that masters a person's life—see 1 Corinthians 6:12.) Admitting our powerlessness over a life-controlling problem(s) or the developing of a life-controlling problem is not a weakness; it is a strength.

We all have the potential for a life-controlling problem(s). Facing the reality of a life-controlling problem may be difficult; however, it is the start on the road to recovery.

Life-controlling problems generally fall into one of three categories: substances, behaviors, and relationships. One of the ways to identify a life-controlling problem (or the start of one) is when a substance, behavior, or relationship interferes in an important area of our life (job, school, family, etc.), and we continue to use, practice, or relate in the same way.

In other words, we are hurting ourselves or others, and we are not changing to correct the destructive issue.

Specify (name) the life-controlling problem with which you are struggling.

In what ways do you feel driven by the problem?

Describe your feelings of hopelessness to manage the problem yourself.

Can you describe an event or situation that has caused you to think more about God in your search for help?

Workbook: *Stepping Into Freedom*, Living Free, P. O. Box 22127, Chattanooga, TN 37422-2127

Session 1

Spiritual-Awareness

Let's look at how the Apostle Paul dealt with powerlessness.

Romans 7:18-20
Paul recognized his own powerlessness.

In what way did Paul show an inability to do good?

How does Paul identify the sinful nature in his inability to do good in himself?

Do you see ways Paul may have been driven by the sinful nature?

Romans 7:21-24
Paul recognized a war in his inner being.

How does Paul describe this war between good and evil?

How do you see his mind being affected?

In what ways can you identify with Paul's being a prisoner in this war with his soul?

Verse 24 shows that the demands of the law and our inability in the flesh place us in a wretched state. The Apostle Paul asked an important question. "Who will rescue me from this body of death?"

Romans 7:25-8:2
Paul recognized that the only way to deal with his powerlessness was through Jesus Christ.

To whom did Paul express his thanks for his rescue from a wretched state?

How does he show that the road to God is through Jesus Christ?

Why do you think he addressed Jesus Christ as his Lord?

How did Paul express his freedom from condemnation?

Application

Paul writes in 2 Corinthians 12:9-10: "But he [Jesus] said to me, 'My grace is sufficient for you, for my power is made perfect in weakness.' Therefore I will boast all the more gladly about my weaknesses, so that Christ's power may rest on me. . . . For when I am weak, then I am strong."

In what ways can you apply these scriptures to your personal struggle(s)?

Additional Scripture References

Psalm 6:6-7 *Proverbs 28:26*
Psalm 31 *Romans 3:9-10, 23*

Step-by-Step Diary

Step 1

 Session 1

Workbook: *Stepping Into Freedom*, Living Free, P. O. Box 22127, Chattanooga, TN 37422-2127

Session 2: *Acknowledging My Belief in Jesus Christ*

Personal Preparation: Getting Ready for Session Two

Step 2 I now realize that my Creator, God the Father, Son, and Holy Spirit, can restore me to wholeness in Christ.

Meet With God

Personal Notes

Take 30 minutes each day to be alone with God in meditation and prayer. Read Philippians 1-4.

Self-Awareness

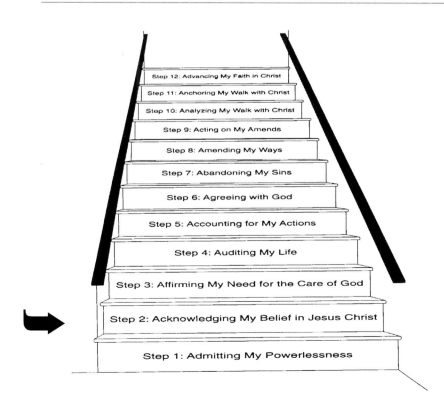

Workbook: *Stepping Into Freedom*, Living Free, P. O. Box 22127, Chattanooga, TN 37422-2127

Session 2

To effectively deal with a life-controlling problem(s), a person needs help from a greater power. This higher power is Jesus Christ, the Son of God. We have access to God only through Jesus Christ, His Son (see John 14:6). It is likely that at some point in your life you have placed your trust in your self-will, a false belief system, or in your own ability to manage your life. It is possible that you may have had unpleasant experiences with Christians and/or developed a distorted concept of God.

Some people see God as only for the weak or sick. Others may be dealing with anger toward God. The most important thing to remember is—there is hope for all in Christ.

Describe ways that you have tried to manage your life.

Describe resources that you have used to manage your life.

Describe the feelings that have come from trying to deal with a life-controlling problem within the sphere of your own strength.

Wholeness in Christ will help you deal with delusion.

As we follow Christ and are obedient to His word, truth will overcome delusion. "Your word is a lamp to my feet and a light for my path" (Psalm 119:105).

Spiritual-Awareness

Now we will look at how God works in us to fulfill His purpose for our lives.

Philippians 2:12-13
Paul encourages his friends to work out their salvation "with fear and trembling" (v12).

What are some of the ways we can work out our salvation as God works in us?

Why is it important to practice reverence (*fear and trembling*) for God (v12)?

Paul emphasizes God's continuing work in us (v13).

In what ways is God working in you?

What are some of the things you are doing (*continue to work out your salvation*) in response to God's work in you?

How do you view God's will and purpose in your life? (See Romans 12:2.)

Workbook: *Stepping Into Freedom*, Living Free, P. O. Box 22127, Chattanooga, TN 37422-2127

Session 2

Romans 10:9-10
Exercising faith in Jesus Christ is vital for salvation (v9).

What does it mean to you to confess with your mouth that Jesus is Lord?

What does it mean to you to "believe in your heart that God raised him [Jesus] from the dead" (v9)?

What is the result of confessing with your mouth that Jesus is Lord and believing in your heart that God raised Jesus from the dead?

Describe the role of the heart and the mouth in verse 10.

Can you describe a time when it was difficult for you to place your trust in Christ?

Psalm 46:1
God—"an ever-present help in trouble."

What comfort does this verse give you?

How do you picture God as your refuge?

Application

God works from the inside out (as He works in us, we work out our salvation). Identify your goals on the chart below.

Identifying Goals

Goals for My:	My Part	God's Part
Church		
Family		
Career		
Personal Needs		
Education		
Physical Needs		
	My Responsibility "Continue to work out your salvation with fear and trembling" (Philippians 2:12).	**God's Responsibility** "For it is God who works in you to will and to act according to his good purpose" (Philippians 2:13).

How would you describe your relationship with Jesus Christ?

Additional Scripture References		
Psalm 27:4-5	Mark 9:23-24	Romans 8:9
Psalm 34:18-22	Mark 10:26-27	2 Corinthians 1:9
Isaiah 12:2	John 8:32	Ephesians 3:20
Ezekiel 36:27	John 15:5	Hebrews 11:6

Step-by-Step Diary

Step 2

Workbook: *Stepping Into Freedom*, Living Free, P. O. Box 22127, Chattanooga, TN 37422-2127

Session 3: Affirming My Need for the Care of God

Personal Preparation: Getting Ready for Session Three

Step 3 I now make a conscious decision to turn my entire will and life over to the care and direction of Jesus Christ as Teacher, Healer, Saviour, and Lord.

Meet With God

Personal Notes

Take 30 minutes each day to be alone with God in meditation and prayer. Read Romans 12-14.

Self-Awareness

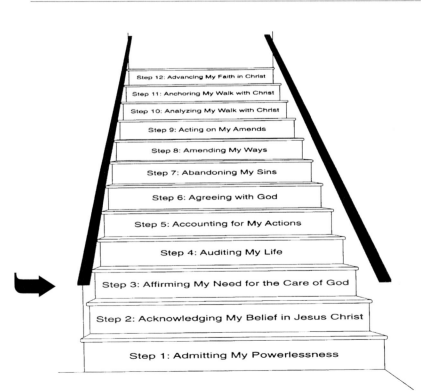

Workbook: *Stepping Into Freedom*, Living Free, P. O. Box 22127, Chattanooga, TN 37422-2127

In this session may you be encouraged to affirm your decision to turn your entire life over to God through Jesus Christ. This step is commitment:

1. To turn your will and life over to God.
2. To decide not to be mastered by any substance, behavior, or personal relationship.
3. To turn control over to the care of God.

In what ways have you resisted God's will for your life?

Describe an area (or areas) in your life that has led to obsessive and/or destructive behaviors.

How difficult is it for you to give up control of your life?

What areas of your life are the most difficult to turn over to the care of God?

Spiritual-Awareness

Let us look at what the Scripture says concerning the surrendering of our will and the direction of our lives to the care of God.

Romans 12:1-2
Having a merciful and compassionate God, we should present our bodies as living sacrifices as a "spiritual act of worship" (v1).

Why do you think Paul describes this as being holy and pleasing to God?

What does a living sacrifice mean to you?

Romans 12:2
We are to guard against being conformed to the ways of this world.

In what ways have you felt pressure to conform to the "pattern of this world"?

Our minds need to be renewed.

In what ways is the transformation of the mind a process?

The Lord has a good and perfect will for everyone. According to Paul, we can test and approve God's will for our lives.

What do you think he means?

Proverbs 3:5-6
We are encouraged to trust in the Lord and acknowledge the
Lord in all our ways.

**In what ways have you depended "on your own understand-
ing" (v5)?**

**How are you acknowledging the Lord for His direction in your
life?**

What do you expect from the Lord?

Psalm 118:8-9
We are encouraged to turn our lives over to the care of God.
This is significant because we choose to "take refuge in the
LORD" (v8) rather than man and even princes (people of
fame).

Application

A meaningful decision requires action on our part.

What actions will accompany your decision to turn your life over to the care of God?

Additional Scripture References		
Joshua 1:8-9	*Jeremiah 29:11-14*	*John 10:29-30*
Proverbs 16:3	*Jeremiah 32:27*	*John 14:6*
Isaiah 30:15	*Mark 10:27*	*Galatians 2:20*
Isaiah 55:6-7	*John 1:12-13*	*Revelation 3:20*

Step-by-Step Diary

Step 3

Workbook: *Stepping Into Freedom*, Living Free, P. O. Box 22127, Chattanooga, TN 37422-2127

Session 4: Auditing My Life

Personal Preparation: Getting Ready for Session Four

Step 4 Having made this decision, I now obey God's call in Scripture to make a fearless, ethical, moral, and scriptural inventory of my entire life in order to uncover all sins, mistakes, and character defects and to make a written list of every item uncovered.

Meet With God

Personal Notes

Take 30 minutes each day to be alone with God in meditation and prayer. Read Psalm 139-150.

Self-Awareness

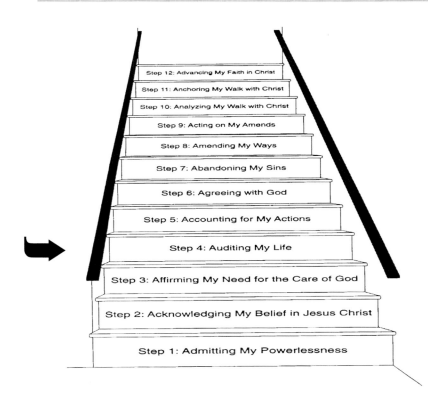

Session 4

Workbook: *Stepping Into Freedom*, Living Free, P. O. Box 22127, Chattanooga, TN 37422-2127

Let us continue to give emphasis to steps 1 through 3 which are the building blocks for recovery. In this step, an emphasis is placed on personal inventory.

May we search with honesty all aspects of our life without the use of excuses for our inappropriate behavior. As we report our personal histories of life-controlling problems, God will be our guide. It is important that we do the written list of thoughts (*Personal Audit*—page 32).

In what ways have you denied the reality of your condition?

Describe ways you have blamed people, circumstances, situations, etc., for your condition.

Discuss ways your behavior has affected other people (family, friends, etc.).

In what ways can a personal examination help you look to God for help?

Workbook: *Stepping Into Freedom*, Living Free, P. O. Box 22127, Chattanooga, TN 37422-2127

Session 4

Personal Audit

My relationship with God:

My relationship with my family:

My relationship with my church:

My relationship with my friends:

Spiritual-Awareness

Let us look at how God encourages each of us to take a personal inventory of our life. Although experiencing the grieving process through repentance is healthy, we should focus on our new hope in Christ. Christ is our only hope as savior, healer, and teacher. He will not disappoint us in our time of personal searching.

Psalm 139:1-2
The Lord knows us personally.

What is your understanding of God's knowing you on a personal basis?

What do you think David means in verse 2, "You know when I sit and when I rise; you perceive my thoughts from afar"?

Psalm 139:3-4
The Lord knows our actions.

How does it make you feel knowing that God is aware of all our ways and even our words before they are spoken?

Psalm 139:23-24
David was open to personal examination.

How do you feel about God's searching our hearts and testing our thoughts?

In what ways can offensive motives deter God's leading in our lives?

Lamentations 3:40
Restoration includes personal examination and testing.

Why is it important to "examine our ways and test them"?

Jeremiah 17:9-10
Jeremiah describes the heart as deceitful.

In what ways can a deceitful heart support our denial of a life-controlling problem?

King David was a man who failed God yet was willing to repent and conduct a personal inventory of his life. He is described as a man after God's own heart (Acts 13:22).

What lessons can we learn from David in conducting our personal inventory?

Additional Scripture References	
Jeremiah 23:24	John 16:13
Lamentations 3:19-23	Romans 8:26-27
John 6:68-69	2 Corinthians 13:5-6
John 14:26	James 1:12

Step-by-Step Diary

Step 4

Workbook: *Stepping Into Freedom*, Living Free, P. O. Box 22127, Chattanooga, TN 37422-2127

Session 5: Accounting for My Actions

Personal Preparation: Getting Ready for Session Five

Step 5 After completing this inventory, I now will to "walk in the light, as he is in the light" by admitting to myself, to God, and to at least one other person in Christ the exact nature of these wrongs.

Meet With God

Personal Notes

Take 30 minutes each day to be alone with God in meditation and prayer. Read 1 John 1-5.

Self-Awareness

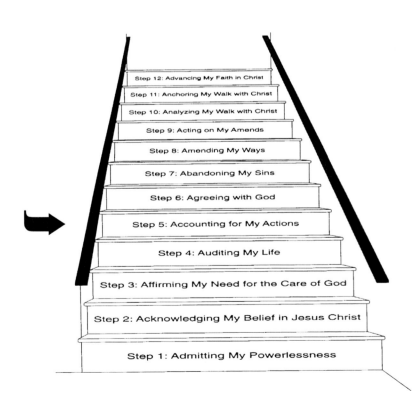

Step 12: Advancing My Faith in Christ
Step 11: Anchoring My Walk with Christ
Step 10: Analyzing My Walk with Christ
Step 9: Acting on My Amends
Step 8: Amending My Ways
Step 7: Abandoning My Sins
Step 6: Agreeing with God
→ Step 5: Accounting for My Actions
Step 4: Auditing My Life
Step 3: Affirming My Need for the Care of God
Step 2: Acknowledging My Belief in Jesus Christ
Step 1: Admitting My Powerlessness

Session 5 — Workbook: *Stepping Into Freedom*, Living Free, P. O. Box 22127, Chattanooga, TN 37422-2127

In this session we will discuss admitting to ourselves, God, and others our thoughts which we prepared on paper in Session 4. Sharing with others helps remove us from the isolation which was caused by a wall of defenses. We use these defenses to protect ourselves from more sorrow from the life-controlling problem(s). We should only share those things that we feel comfortable in sharing with the other group members.

Although it may be helpful for us to share our concerns with another person who is mature in Christ, only Christ can forgive sins. There may be some personal concerns that *only God needs to know.*

Working within your personal comfort level, what are those items from your written list of wrongs prepared in Session 4 (see Personal Audit, page 32) that you wish to report?

In what ways have you experienced isolation due to a life-controlling problem?

Describe the type of person with whom you prefer to talk about your problem.

Admitting the exact nature of my wrongs to myself and others is important.

Why is it more important to admit our wrongs to God?

Workbook: *Stepping Into Freedom*, Living Free, P. O. Box 22127, Chattanooga, TN 37422-2127   Session 5 **37**

Spiritual-Awareness

Let us look at what the Scripture says about walking "in the light, as he is in the light" (1 John 1:7).

1 John 1:5-6
God is light and truth.

What does the term "in him there is no darkness at all" (v5) mean to you?

What hinders our fellowship with God?

1 John 1:7
Walking in the light results in fellowship with God and one another.

How does walking in the light affect our relationship with other believers?

What is the significance of the blood of Jesus?

1 John 1:8-10
John describes the cause and remedy for deceit.

How do we deceive ourselves?

Why is confession of sin necessary in our walk with God?

Why is denial of sin so destructive to our fellowship with God?

1 John 2:1-2
Jesus is the mediator between God and man.

What comfort and assurance do these verses give us?

James 5:16
Confession and prayer are vital to the healing process.

Since Jesus is the forgiver of our sins, why is confession of faults to one another helpful?

Why is prayer so vital to our walking in the light?

Workbook: *Stepping Into Freedom*, Living Free, P. O. Box 22127, Chattanooga, TN 37422-2127   **Session 5**

Application

The Apostle Paul writes, "He forgave us all our sins, having canceled the written code, with its regulations, that was against us and that stood opposed to us; he took it away, nailing it to the cross" (Colossians 2:13-14).

Since our sins have been forgiven and nailed to the cross, our written list of wrongs (*Personal Audit*) should be destroyed in praise to our God.

What is your prayer of thanksgiving?

There were things on the written list (*Personal Audit*) that can only be dealt with by God. However, there may be items on the list that need continued prayer and corrective action on your part. These can be described on the *Prayer List* on the next page.

Additional Scripture References

Psalm 119:9-11	*Acts 3:19*	*Ephesians 5:13-14*
Proverbs 28:13	*Acts 13:38-39*	*1 Timothy 1:15*
Jeremiah 14:20	*Romans 3:23*	*Hebrews 9:14*
Acts 2:37-38	*Romans 14:12*	

Prayer List

Person and/or Situation	Request

Workbook: *Stepping Into Freedom*, Living Free, P. O. Box 22127, Chattanooga, TN 37422-2127

Step-by-Step Diary

Step 5

Session 5

Workbook: *Stepping Into Freedom*, Living Free, P. O. Box 22127, Chattanooga, TN 37422-2127

Session 6: Agreeing with God

Personal Preparation: Getting Ready for Session Six

Step 6 Having agreed with God about my sinful behavior, I now ask for His forgiveness through Christ and openly acknowledge that I am forgiven according to Scripture.

Meet With God

Personal Notes

Take 30 minutes each day to be alone with God in meditation and prayer. Read James 1-5.

Self-Awareness

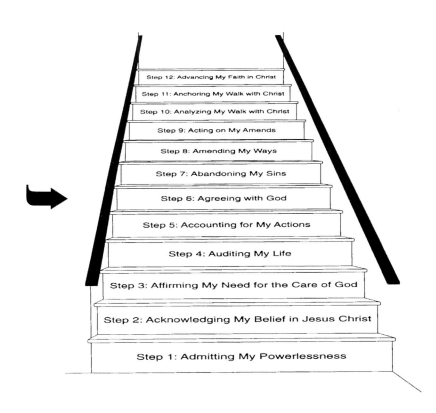

Workbook: *Stepping Into Freedom*, Living Free, P. O. Box 22127, Chattanooga, TN 37422-2127

Session 6

In steps 1-5, emphasis has been placed on building a foundation for change. We have looked at our denial and delusion and asked the Lord to give us clear thinking so we can follow Him. In this session, you will be encouraged to continue your denouncement of sin and focus on *walking out* the changes in your lives.

What behaviors have violated your value system?

Describe the actions you are taking to confront these negative trends of behavior.

How have negative trends of behavior affected your self-esteem?

What areas of self-management have been the most difficult for you to turn over to God?

Session 6

Workbook: *Stepping Into Freedom*, Living Free, P. O. Box 22127, Chattanooga, TN 37422-2127

Spiritual-Awareness

Agreeing with God and walking with God go hand in hand.

Amos 3:3
Walking with God means harmony.

Why is it hard for two to walk together unless they are in agreement?

How do you see your change of behavior as a cooperative effort with the Lord?

James 4:7-8
Walking with God means submission.

What is the promise for those who resist the devil?

James 4:9-10
Walking with God means humility.

What is the promise for those who humble themselves "before the Lord"?

Ephesians 1:7
Walking with God means I agree with God that I am forgiven of my sins.

What does it mean to be freely forgiven of your sins?

What price did Christ pay for this forgiveness?

Jude 21
Read this verse from *The Living Bible*.

How does this verse refer to the blessing of God's boundaries?

Application

What outward changes in your life are happening as a result of your commitment to agree with God, allowing Him to manage your life?

Additional Scripture References		
Psalm 27:13-14	*Proverbs 19:21*	*2 Thessalonians 3:3*
Psalm 37:4-5	*Proverbs 21:30-31*	*Hebrews 4:16*
Psalm 118:17-18	*Isaiah 1:18-19*	
Psalm 119:11	*Romans 6:11-14*	

Step-by-Step Diary

Step 6

Session 6

Workbook: *Stepping Into Freedom*, Living Free, P. O. Box 22127, Chattanooga, TN 37422-2127

Session 7: Abandoning My Sins

Step 7 I now repent (turn away) from all these behaviors in thought, word, and deed and ask God to remove each besetting sin through Jesus Christ.

Personal Preparation: Getting Ready for Session Seven

Meet With God

Take 30 minutes each day to be alone with God in meditation and prayer. Read Hebrews 11-13.

Personal Notes

Self-Awareness

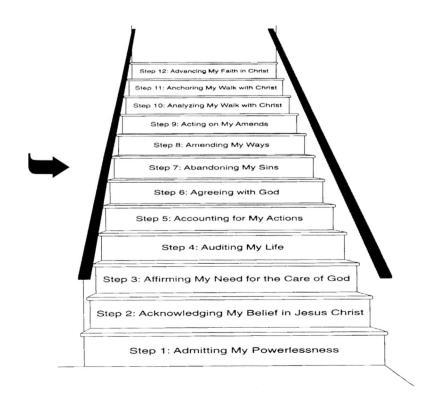

Step 12: Advancing My Faith in Christ
Step 11: Anchoring My Walk with Christ
Step 10: Analyzing My Walk with Christ
Step 9: Acting on My Amends
Step 8: Amending My Ways
→ Step 7: Abandoning My Sins
Step 6: Agreeing with God
Step 5: Accounting for My Actions
Step 4: Auditing My Life
Step 3: Affirming My Need for the Care of God
Step 2: Acknowledging My Belief in Jesus Christ
Step 1: Admitting My Powerlessness

Workbook: *Stepping Into Freedom*, Living Free, P. O. Box 22127, Chattanooga, TN 37422-2127

The emphasis in this session is to continue to "walk out" the changes in our lives. To do this, we must focus on "turning from" our sins.

These shortcomings should be approached with an attitude of surrender. Having confessed them to Christ and others, we must now allow Him to purify us.

What are some of your experiences in "walking out" the changes since the previous meeting?

What are some character issues with which you continue to struggle?

What are some of the struggles you have experienced from the surrender of your life to God?

What is your definition of repentance?

Spiritual-Awareness

Let us look at repentance (turning away) from behaviors and substances that are destructive to God's plan for our life.

Hebrews 12:1
We are encouraged to deal with "everything that hinders" us.

Why do you think the writer of Hebrews refers to "a great cloud of witnesses"?

What relationship is there to the preceding chapter?

In what ways can we become entangled with certain sins?

What does "run with perseverance the race marked out for us" mean to you? In what ways is the Christian life a race?

Hebrews 12:2
We are encouraged to focus our attention on Jesus.

How do you picture Jesus as the source (the author) of your faith?

How do you picture Jesus as the finisher of your faith?

In view of verse 2, what does it mean to you that Jesus "endured the cross"?

Hebrews 12:3
We are encouraged to consider the endurance of Jesus. He received opposition.

What are some ways God is helping you overcome opposition from destructive behaviors?

What comfort do you receive from the encouragement to "not grow weary"?

Acts 26:20
Repentance is proved by one's deeds.

List examples of your actions that are changing based on your "turning to God."

52 Session 7   Workbook: *Stepping Into Freedom*, Living Free, P. O. Box 22127, Chattanooga, TN 37422-2127

Acts 3:19
Repentance brings a refreshing from the Lord.

Describe this verse in your own words.

Acts 20:21
Repentance toward God and faith in the Lord Jesus Christ go hand in hand. There is much emphasis on confession in our society, even in secular circles. However, confession alone is not enough. We must repent and have faith in Jesus Christ. When we trust Christ as our Savior and walk according to His Word, Christ fills the void in our lives that is often felt when a person starts the road to recovery.

Application

Solomon writes, "Trust in the LORD with all your heart and lean not on your own understanding; in all your ways acknowledge him, and he will make your paths straight" (Proverbs 3:5-6).

How do you plan to apply these verses to your life when dealing with hindrances to your walk in Christ?

Additional Scripture References		
Job 11:13-19	*John 5:14*	*2 Corinthians 10:5*
Psalm 51:10	*John 8:10-11*	*Philippians 4:6*
Psalm 90:8	*Romans 5*	*Colossians 3:17*
Psalm 103:2-3	*Romans 6*	*1 Peter 5:6-7*
Ezekiel 18:30-32	*Romans 12:1-2*	*1 John 2:3-6*
Daniel 4:27	*2 Corinthians 2:10*	

Step-by-Step Diary

Step 7

Workbook: *Stepping Into Freedom*, Living Free, P. O. Box 22127, Chattanooga, TN 37422-2127

Session 8: Amending My Ways

Personal Preparation: Getting Ready for Session Eight

Step 8 I now make a list of all persons I have harmed in thought, word, and deed and a list of all persons I believe have harmed me, and I will to make amends to all of them.

Meet With God

Personal Notes

Take 30 minutes each day to be alone with God in meditation and prayer. Read 2 Corinthians 5-9.

Self-Awareness

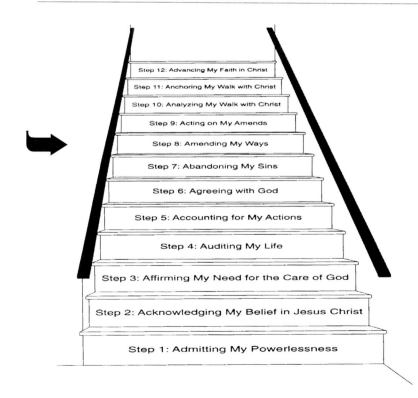

Workbook: *Stepping Into Freedom*, Living Free, P. O. Box 22127, Chattanooga, TN 37422-2127

Session 8   55

As the Lord helps us become aware of the delusion in our lives, we are faced with the reality that others may have been harmed by our behaviors. Continued cover-up or blaming others for our behaviors can result in further delusion and bitterness. Forgiving ourselves and others through Christ helps us overcome the past.

Make a list of persons you have harmed. This is for your own personal reflection. See *Amends* on page 60.

Describe the most urgent relationship that needs to be amended.

In what ways have you tried to cover up for your inappropriate behaviors?

Describe past misdeeds that you cannot correct and have turned over to God.

How does making amends through Christ help free you from the past?

Session 8   Workbook: *Stepping Into Freedom*, Living Free, P. O. Box 22127, Chattanooga, TN 37422-2127

Spiritual-Awareness

Now let us look at what the Scripture says about the ministry of reconciliation.

2 Corinthians 5:17
Being in Christ helps us deal with the past.

What does being "a new creation" mean to you?

How does "the old has gone, the new has come" apply to your life?

2 Corinthians 5:18
Reconciliation comes through Christ.

What does reconciliation *through Christ* mean to you?

How do you view "the ministry of reconciliation"?

2 Corinthians 5:19
Our sins are not held against us.

How does it make you feel knowing that the sins of the past have been forgiven?

How do you feel about God committing to you "the message of reconciliation"?

How do you express this in view of broken relationships?

2 Corinthians 5:20
We are ambassadors for Christ.

What is your view of an ambassador of Christ?

Why do you think Paul focuses on Christ as the key to reconciliation with God?

2 Corinthians 5:21
Our identity is in Christ.

How do you picture the sinless Christ becoming sin for us?

What does it mean to you that in Christ we "become the righteousness of God"?

Matthew 6:14-15; Colossians 3:13
Unforgiveness of ourselves and others hinders our relationship with God and others. We cannot be in a right relationship with God and in an unforgiving relationship with others.

How is the importance of forgiveness emphasized in these passages?

Matthew 18:21-35
These verses tell what will happen to a person who chooses not to forgive.

What will happen to such an individual?

Session 8 — Workbook: *Stepping Into Freedom*, Living Free, P. O. Box 22127, Chattanooga, TN 37422-2127

Application

In view of Jesus' statement, "Do to others as you would have them do to you" (Luke 6:31), how do you plan your approach in amending broken or strained relationships?

Additional Scripture References

Leviticus 19:17-18 *Hosea 11:1-4* *Ephesians 4:29-32*
Psalm 19:13-14 *Matthew 5:9, 43-45* *1 John 4:7-12*
Psalm 32:1-2 *Mark 12:31*

Amends

Person	Relationship	Actions to Correct

Session 8

Workbook: *Stepping Into Freedom*, Living Free, P. O. Box 22127, Chattanooga, TN 37422-2127

Step-by-Step Diary

Step 8

Workbook: *Stepping Into Freedom*, Living Free, P. O. Box 22127, Chattanooga, TN 37422-2127

Session 9: Acting on My Amends

Personal Preparation: Getting Ready for Session Nine

Step 9 I now go directly to these persons to forgive and to seek forgiveness, reconciliation, restitution, or release whenever and with whomever possible, unless to do so would cause further harm.

Meet With God

Personal Notes

Take 30 minutes each day to be alone with God in meditation and prayer. Read Matthew 5-7 and Luke 15.

Self-Awareness

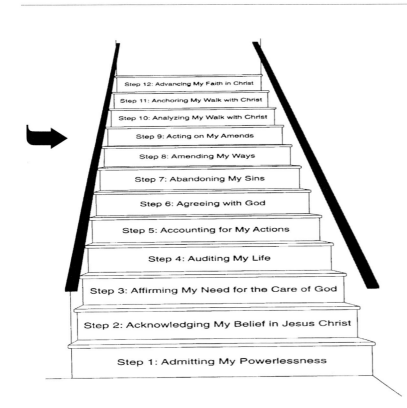

Session 9

Workbook: *Stepping Into Freedom*, Living Free, P. O. Box 22127, Chattanooga, TN 37422-2127

The general goal of this session is to encourage each other to go to those who may have been harmed by strained or broken relationships. It is important to use wisdom in seeking forgiveness and reconciliation. Approach only those to whom you have access and would not cause further harm (further harm includes areas that may cause damage which would be beyond repair). The purpose is to reconcile, not to document the other person's mistakes or to blame others.

Describe strained or broken relationships with people who are approachable and with whom making amends would not cause further harm.

Describe former harmful relationships with people who are no longer approachable (because the person is deceased or because of concern for further harm).

How are you turning your inaccessible, strained, or broken relationships which cannot be further dealt with over to God?

Workbook: *Stepping Into Freedom*, Living Free, P. O. Box 22127, Chattanooga, TN 37422-2127

Describe your present feelings about your peace with God.

Spiritual-Awareness

Let us look at the Scripture to see how to make restitution and/or release to the Lord those relationships which cannot be restored because of inaccessibility or likelihood of further harm.

Matthew 5:23-24
We are encouraged to make peace with our brother.

Describe these verses in your own words.

In your times of prayer and meditation, have you been reminded of strained and broken relationships? Describe.

In what ways can you apply these verses to your strained or broken relationships?

Luke 15:18-21
The prodigal son made peace with his father and heaven.

What action did this son take to make peace with his father and heaven?

Why was it important for him to admit his sin against his father and heaven?

How do you picture the son's humility?

Describe the reconciliation of the father and son in your own words.

It is important to take responsibility for our own actions wherever possible. We can be comforted with the assurance that God helps us with those broken relationships that are beyond our control. Peter says, "Cast all your anxiety on him because he cares for you" (1 Peter 5:7).

Application

Describe difficult situations you might face in your effort to make amends.

In what ways can this group help you?

In what ways can you help support others in this group?

Additional Scripture References

Numbers 5:5-7	*Luke 6:35*	*1 Thessalonians 5:11*
Isaiah 1:18-20	*Romans 12:17-18*	*Ephesians 5:21*
Ezekiel 33:15-16	*Philippians 2:3-4*	

Step-by-Step Diary

Step 9

Workbook: *Stepping Into Freedom*, Living Free, P. O. Box 22127, Chattanooga, TN 37422-2127

Session 10: Analyzing My Walk with Christ

Personal Preparation: Getting Ready for Session Ten

Step 10 I now consciously and prayerfully continue to "walk in the light" by unceasingly taking personal inventory of all my temptations and sins, and by keeping a constantly open relationship with God, myself, and other persons.

Meet With God

Personal Notes

Take 30 minutes each day to be alone with God in meditation and prayer. Read 1 Corinthians 10 and 2 Corinthians 1-3.

Self-Awareness

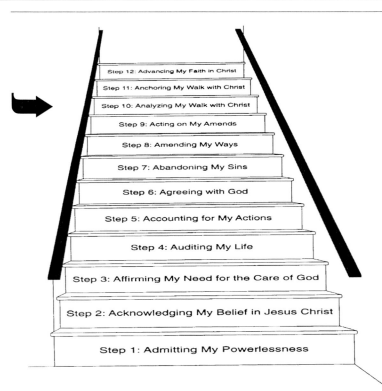

Step 12: Advancing My Faith in Christ
Step 11: Anchoring My Walk with Christ
→ Step 10: Analyzing My Walk with Christ
Step 9: Acting on My Amends
Step 8: Amending My Ways
Step 7: Abandoning My Sins
Step 6: Agreeing with God
Step 5: Accounting for My Actions
Step 4: Auditing My Life
Step 3: Affirming My Need for the Care of God
Step 2: Acknowledging My Belief in Jesus Christ
Step 1: Admitting My Powerlessness

In this session we will focus on maintaining the gains we have made to this point. It is helpful to discuss our victories, but we also need to be aware of our weaknesses to relapse into our former lifestyle.

Describe the gains you have made to remain free of life-controlling problems.

What are some of the triggering devices you must guard against which can lead to relapse?

What does an open relationship with God mean to you (See 1 John 1:7)?

Workbook: *Stepping Into Freedom*, Living Free, P. O. Box 22127, Chattanooga, TN 37422-2127

Session 10

Spiritual-Awareness

We will look at the Scripture as it relates to being confident in Christ (not in our own accomplishments) and of being open before the Lord about the temptations which can hinder our walk with Christ.

1 Corinthians 10:12
Paul warns against being overconfident.

Why do you think Paul warns us about falling?

How can you relate to this verse?

1 Corinthians 10:13
Paul shows how to deal with temptation.

Why is your temptation not unique?

Describe God's part in helping you with temptation.

Describe your responsibility in dealing with temptation.

2 Corinthians 3:4-6
Our confidence should be in Christ, not in our own resources.

In what ways can you apply these verses to your life?

How do you think God makes us "competent as ministers" (v6)?

James 1:13-15
God does not tempt us.

In view of these verses, describe what can happen if you give in to temptation.

An open relationship with God is the key to dealing with overconfidence and temptations. It is important to be honest with God (Luke 18:13), self (Romans 12:3), and others (2 Samuel 12:13).

Application

Describe your progress at this point.

Additional Scripture References		
139:1-4	Galatians 6:4-5	Psalm 4:3-5 Psalm
Psalm 34:12-14	Proverbs 30:8-9	Ephesians 4:25-26

Workbook: *Stepping Into Freedom*, Living Free, P. O. Box 22127, Chattanooga, TN 37422-2127

Step-by-Step Diary

Step 10

Session 10

Workbook: *Stepping Into Freedom*, Living Free, P. O. Box 22127, Chattanooga, TN 37422-2127

Session 11: Anchoring My Walk with Christ

Personal Preparation: Getting Ready for Session Eleven

Step 11 I now continue in regular Scripture study, prayer, worship, and fellowship to increase God's will in my life.

Meet With God

Personal Notes

Take 30 minutes each day to be alone with God in meditation and prayer. Read Colossians 1-4.

Self-Awareness

Step 12: Advancing My Faith in Christ
Step 11: Anchoring My Walk with Christ
Step 10: Analyzing My Walk with Christ
Step 9: Acting on My Amends
Step 8: Amending My Ways
Step 7: Abandoning My Sins
Step 6: Agreeing with God
Step 5: Accounting for My Actions
Step 4: Auditing My Life
Step 3: Affirming My Need for the Care of God
Step 2: Acknowledging My Belief in Jesus Christ
Step 1: Admitting My Powerlessness

Workbook: *Stepping Into Freedom*, Living Free, P. O. Box 22127, Chattanooga, TN 37422-2127

This session is a continuation of Session 10. Turning our lives over to the care of God and dealing with our character defects are important in living free of life-controlling problems.

Now the challenge is to continue to walk out these changes. Regular times of prayer and meditation will help direct our thoughts on God and His will for our lives.

How are you dealing with negative thoughts? See Philippians 4:8.

Why is it important not to permit negative thoughts to linger in our minds? See Mark 7:21-23.

Describe your personal need to meditate on God and His word. See Joshua 1:8.

Garth Lean in his book, *On the Tail of a Comet,* writes extensively about the life of Frank Buchman. Buchman's principles of change were instrumental in the starting of the Alcoholics Anonymous movement. Lean writes:

> Buchman had learnt that temptation, of whatever kind, was best resisted at its earliest stage. It was easier, he sometimes said, to divert a small stream than to dam a river. He defined the progression of temptation as the look, the thought, the fascination, the fall, and said that the time to deal with it was at the thought—tackle temptation well upstream (80).

In what ways is God influencing your daily inventory of thoughts and actions?

Spiritual-Awareness

God directs our lives on a daily basis through prayer, study, and meditation of His word.

Colossians 3:12
As God's chosen people, we are to clothe ourselves with His garments.

As God's representatives, in what ways are we to clothe ourselves? Describe in your own words.

Colossians 3:13
Paul emphasizes forgiveness.

What does "bear with each other" mean to you?

Who is our example for forgiveness?

Describe what Christ's example of forgiveness means to you?

Colossians 3:14
Love and perfect unity go hand in hand.

What does "put on love" mean to you?

What part does love play in bringing unity among believers?

Colossians 3:15
The "peace of Christ" plays an important role in directing our lives.

What role does the "peace of Christ" play?

Why do you think Paul encourages us to be thankful?

How can you apply this verse to your life?

Colossians 3:16
We are encouraged to "let the word of Christ dwell in [us]."

In what ways do you picture the "word of Christ" being the foundation of Christian activities listed in this verse?

Why do you think Paul emphasizes "gratitude in your hearts to God"?

Colossians 3:17
We are encouraged to do all "in the name of the Lord Jesus."

How can you apply this verse to your life?

Session 11

Workbook: *Stepping Into Freedom*, Living Free, P. O. Box 22127, Chattanooga, TN 37422-2127

Application

Describe your present schedule for your personal devotions.

How do you feel about persistence with your personal devotions?

How do you deal with interruptions?

Is there a glaring weakness in your personal devotional life the Lord is showing you? Describe the weakness and your resolve to correct this very important spiritual aspect of your life.

Additional Scripture References

Joshua 1:8	*Psalm 63:1-7*	*Mark 11:24*
1 Kings 8:56-61	*Psalm 89:15*	*Mark 12:28-33*
Psalm 1:1-3	*Isaiah 30:21*	*Acts 2:42*
Psalm 19:14	*Matthew 6:33-34*	*Philippians 4:6-9*
Psalm 25:1-5	*Matthew 7:7*	

Step-by-Step Diary

Step 11

Session 11

Workbook: *Stepping Into Freedom*, Living Free, P. O. Box 22127, Chattanooga, TN 37422-2127

Session 12: Advancing My Faith in Christ

Personal Preparation: Getting Ready for Session Twelve

Step 12 Recognizing the impact of God in my life, I now intentionally share these principles and their effect with others as God's Spirit leads, and will to practice these principles in all areas of my life.

Meet With God

Personal Notes

Take 30 minutes each day to be alone with God in meditation and prayer. Read 1 Peter 1-5.

Self-Awareness

Workbook: *Stepping Into Freedom*, Living Free, P. O. Box 22127, Chattanooga, TN 37422-2127

This session brings us to a point of completion; however, our spiritual walk with Christ is not complete. As we continue to walk out the truths learned and applied in this course, we should place our focus on reaching out to others who need our help.

The general goal of this session is for each group member to encourage one another to share with others the principles learned in this bible study. As you share with others what the Lord has done in your life, your confidence will be enhanced.

Describe reasons why you feel responsible to share with others the principles you have learned.

In what ways do you feel free to share with others since God has helped you with a struggle and/or stronghold?

Do you have any anxiety about sharing with others? Describe.

Describe a significant person(s) God used in helping you. In what ways did this person(s) help you?

Spiritual-Awareness

Peter encourages us to share the hope we have in Christ. We should always be prepared to share our faith with others.

1 Peter 3:15
Christ should have a special place in our hearts.

What do you think Peter means by "in your hearts set apart Christ as Lord"?

According to this verse, we should be prepared "to give the reason for the hope" we have.

When should we be prepared?

Upon what is our hope based? See Colossians 1:27 and Hebrews 6:19-20.

Why do you think Peter encourages us to share our hope "with gentleness and respect"?

Give examples of opportunities where we can share "with gentleness and respect."

1 Peter 3:16
We are to maintain "a clear conscience."

Sharing our faith with gentleness and respect along with a clear conscience is important. In view of this verse, why is it important?

1 Peter 3:17
God's will for our lives may include suffering.

Can you think of ways you have suffered for doing good? For doing evil?

What is the difference between suffering for good and suffering for evil?

1 Peter 3:18
Christ died for our sins.

Describe in your own words the significance of "Christ died for sins once for all."

In view of this verse, why did He die for our sins?

How was He made alive?

Proverbs 24:11; Jude 22-25
We are to help those being led to the way of death. There are two good things that happen when we share our faith in Christ:
1. We show those being led to the way of death that there is new life in Him.
2. We are always enriched by this experience of sharing our faith in our Savior.

Session 12

Workbook: *Stepping Into Freedom*, Living Free, P. O. Box 22127, Chattanooga, TN 37422-2127

Application

Paul writes, "Praise be to the God and Father of our Lord Jesus Christ, the Father of compassion and the God of all comfort, who comforts us in all our troubles, so that we can comfort those in any trouble with the comfort we ourselves have received from God" (2 Corinthians 1:3-4).

What is your plan to comfort others "with the comfort we ourselves have received from God"?

Why do you think it is important to share the comfort we have received from the Lord?

How will you depend upon the Holy Spirit to guide you? Describe.

Additional Scripture References

Psalm 40:8-10	*Mark 5:19*	*Ephesians 5:8-10*
Isaiah 61:1-3	*Luke 4:18-19*	*Ephesians 6:10-18*
Jeremiah 20:9	*2 Corinthians 3:17-18*	*Colossians 4:5-6*
Micah 6:8	*Galatians 5:1*	*Revelation 12:11*
Matthew 28:19-20	*Galatians 6:1-5*	

Complete the *Follow-Up: Where Do I Go from Here?* on pages 84-85

Follow-Up: Where Do I Go from Here?

Goal Setting

1. **Three Goals for My Life**

   A.

   B.

   C.

2. **Submitting My Goals to God's Care and Direction**

   Trust in the LORD with all your heart and lean not on your own understanding; in all your ways acknowledge him, and he will make your paths straight (Proverbs 3:5-6).

   Ways I will trust the Lord and lean on Him for understanding to achieve my goals:

   Goal A:

   Goal B:

   Goal C:

Ways I will acknowledge Him to direct my life to achieve my goals:

Goal A:

Goal B:

Goal C:

3. **Areas I Need to Work on to Achieve My Goals**

Goal A:

Goal B:

Goal C:

4. **I Recognize That God's Purpose for My Life May Change My Goals**

Many are the plans in a man's heart, but it is the LORD's purpose that prevails (Proverbs 19:21).

My Prayer of Submission:

Memory Verse

"For I know the plans I have for you," declares the LORD, "plans to prosper you and not to harm you, plans to give you hope and a future" **(Jeremiah 29:11).**

Step-by-Step Diary

Step12

Session 12

Workbook: *Stepping Into Freedom*, Living Free, P. O. Box 22127, Chattanooga, TN 37422-2127

References

Ackerman, Robert J. *Children of Alcoholics: A Guidebook for Educators, Therapists, and Parents.* Holmes Beach, FL: Learning Publications, 1978.

Apthorp, Stephen P. *Alcohol and Substance Abuse.* Wilton, CT: Morehouse-Barlow, 1985.

Augsburger, David. *Caring Enough to Confront.* Glendale: Regal, 1980.

Beattie, Melody. *Codependent No More.* New York: Harper and Row, 1988.

Benner, David G. (ed.). *Psychotherapy in Christian Perspective.* Grand Rapids: Baker, 1987.

Carnes, Patrick. *Out of the Shadows: Understanding Sexual Addiction.* Minneapolis: CompCare Publishers, 1983.

Crabb, Lawrence J. *Effective Biblical Counseling.* Grand Rapids: Zondervan, 1977.

George, Carl F. *The Coming Church Revolution.* Grand Rapids: Revell, 1994.

Hart, Archibald D. *Adrenalin and Stress.* Dallas: Word, 1991.

_____. *Counseling the Depressed.* Dallas: Word, 1987.

Johnson, Vernon E. *I'll Quit Tomorrow.* San Francisco: Harper and Row, 1980.

Krupnick, Louis B., and Elizabeth Krupnick. *From Despair to Decision.* Minneapolis: CompCare, 1985.

Lean, Garth. *On the Tail of a Comet.* Colorado Springs: Helmers and Howard, 1985.

Lee, Jimmy Ray. *Understanding the Times.* Chattanooga: Living Free Ministries, Inc. 1997.

_____. *Godly Heroes.* Chattanooga: Living Free Ministries, Inc. 1997.

May, Gerald G. *Addiction and Grace.* San Francisco: Harper and Row Publishers, 1988.

Matzat, Don. *Christ-Esteem.* Eugene: Harvest House, 1990.

McGee, Robert S. *Father Hunger.* Ann Arbor: Servant Publications, 1993.

Menninger, Karl. *Whatever Became of Sin?* New York: Hawthorn, 1973.

Miller, J. Keith. *Sin: Overcoming the Ultimate Deadly Addiction.* San Francisco: Harper and Row, 1987.

Minirth, Frank, et al. *Taking Control.* Grand Rapids: Baker, 1988.

_____. *Love Hunger.* Nashville: Thomas Nelson Publishers, 1990.

O'Gorman, Patricia, and Philip Oliver-Diaz. *Breaking the Cycle of Addiction.* Deerfield Beach: Health Communications, 1987.

Patterson, James, and Peter Kim. *The Day America Told the Truth.* New York: Penguin Books, 1992.

Perkins, Bill. *Fatal Attractions.* Eugene: Harvest House, 1991.

Schaumburg, Harry W. *False Intimacy.* Colorado Springs: Navpress, 1997.

Twerski, Abraham. *Addictive Thinking.* New York: Harper and Row, 1990.

VanVonderen, Jeffrey. *Good News for the Chemically Dependent.* Nashville: Thomas Nelson, 1985.

Workbook: *Stepping Into Freedom*, Living Free, P. O. Box 22127, Chattanooga, TN 37422-2127

Workbook: *Stepping Into Freedom*, Living Free, P. O. Box 22127, Chattanooga, TN 37422-2127